Rogue River

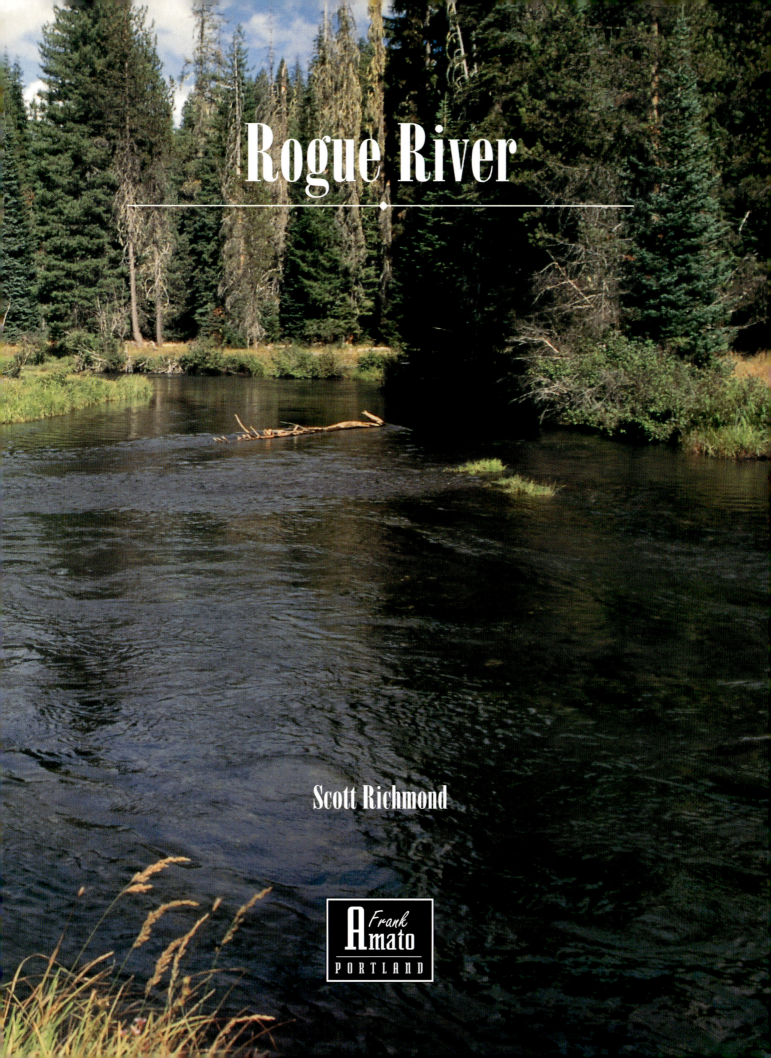

Rogue River

Scott Richmond

Frank Amato
PORTLAND

Volume 6, Number 1

◆

Acknowledgments

Mike St. John for insights on steelheading and good times fishing together. Ron Tenison for salmon. Gary Kraus and Sterling Becklin for the Illinois. Dennis Becklin for the relationship between streamflow and anadromous fish populations. Al Brunnell for half-pounders and lower river. Dave Roberts for trout. Cindy Ricks of the US Forest Service for geology. Dave Haight of the Oregon Dept. of Fish and Wildlife for biology. Craig Fox for steelhead flies. Kenny Moorish of Ashland Outdoor Store and Jay Daley of McKenzie Outfitters for general information and support.

Series Editor: Frank Amato
Kim Koch

Photography: Scott Richmond (unless otherwise noted)
Fly plates photographed by: Jim Schollmeyer
Design: Tony Amato
Map: Tony Amato

Softbound ISBN: 1-57188-171-9; Hardbound ISBN: 1-57188-172-7
(Hardbound edition limited to 350-500 copies)

Rogue River

List of Access Points (from Lost Creek Lake to Mouth)

1. Holy Water
2. Hatchery (ramp)
3. McGregor Park/Bridge Hole
4. Rogue Elk (ramp, camping)
5. Shady Cove Park (camping)
6. Takelma (ramp)
7. Dodge Bridge (ramp)
8. Modoc
9. Touvelle Park (ramp)

10. Gold Nugget
11. Gold Hill Park (ramp)
12. Sardone Creek
13. Valley of the Rogue St. Park (ramp/camping)
14. Coyote Evans/Dee's Landing (ramp)/Fleming
15. Savage Rapids Park
16. Pierce Riffle (ramp)

17. Chinook Park (ramp)
18. Tom Pearce Park
19. Baker Park (ramp)
20. Riverside Park (ramp)
21. Water Restoration
22. Tussing Park
23. Schroeder (ramp)
24. Lathrop (ramp)
25. Whitehorse (ramp/camping)

26. Matson Park
27. Griffin Park (camp)
28. Ferry Park
29. Robertson Bridge (ramp)
30. Hog Creek (ramp)
31. Indian Mary (ramp, camping)
32. Rainbow
33. Ennis Riffle (ramp)

34. Carpenter Island
35. Galice Creek
36. Galice (ramp)
37. Chair Riffle
38. Rand (ramp)
39. Alameda (ramp/camping)
40. Argo (ramp)
41. Grave Creek (ramp)

42. Foster Bar
43. Bill Moore Creek
44. Quosatana (ramp/campground)
45. Lobster Cr. (ramp/camping)
46. Orchard Bar
47. Huntley Park (campground)
48. Coyote Bar
49. Plywood Mill

Upper Rogue 1-9   **Upper Middle Rogue** 10-15   **Lower Middle Rogue** 16-41   **Lower Rogue** 42-49

Rogue River

◆

Ron Tenison looked at the nine-weight Sage rod in his right hand, then at the seven-weight in his left hand. "Salmon or steelhead. Salmon or steelhead," he said, alternately lifting the two rods. "Steelhead," he said with finality. He leaned the nine-weight against a willow and headed for the river with the lighter rig. It was a rational decision for early July on the Rogue River. The big push of spring chinook was over, and summer steelhead were beginning to show up.

Ron cast to a slot on one side of the island, while I headed for the other side. I'd only gone a few steps when I heard the sound of a reel spinning at high rpm. Ron was leaning back, his rod in a deep arc, line zipping upriver. I turned back and went to watch the fun.

"I'm hosed," Ron said through clenched teeth. His fish surfaced, showing huge slab sides. "Twenty-five pounds, at least. Probably a wild springer."

"You're hosed," I agreed. Although the current was strong, the big spring chinook salmon ripped upriver like a Ferrari across Nevada. Backing melted from the spool. "Definitely hosed," I said. "Wrong rod."

A short section of black-tinted backing shot through the guides. "Only fifty feet left," Ron said. The fish hadn't slowed a bit. "Definitely hosed." He pointed the rod at the fish and palmed the reel. The line stretched tight, then went limp. Ron reeled up and shrugged. "Wrong rod."

The Rogue River can be a confusing place for fly anglers. Fresh anadromous fish enter the river every month of the year. Early-arriving spring salmon swim with the last of the winter steelhead. Summer steelhead head upriver cheek-to-jowl with the end of the spring salmon. The first fall chinook not far behind. Coho salmon swim beside the first of the winter steelhead. If that's not enough, there's a fly-fishing-only tailwater that offers year-round angling for resident rainbows that can go five pounds or more. And in summer, both browns and rainbows can be found in the headwaters. Each day, an angler has to decide which outstanding opportunity to take advantage of. That's life in the Rogue Country.

Collisions

For millions of years, a rocky island in the Pacific Ocean drifted slowly eastward, carried along by the crustal plate it was part of. As it traveled, the island scraped up sediments from the sea floor and bits of the ocean's crust. About 250 million years ago, the whole mess collided with the North American continent. Over the next 100 million years, six more islands slammed into each other like tectonic bumper cars and welded themselves to the continent. Those islands are now called the Klamath Mountains. The Rogue River cuts a path to the sea through them.

The sea floor that brought the islands continued to move eastward, sinking beneath the accreted landmasses. Eventually it reached deep enough into the earth that it melted and created a vast reservoir of molten rock. About 38 million years ago, this liquid rock began to push to the surface. Over the next 20 million years, volcanic vents released basalt that spread over the land, creating the broad mounds that make up the Western Cascades.

Sometimes fall steelhead anglers are surprised by a chinook salmon, such as this 15-pounder that picked up a size-12 Big Bird.

At Rogue River Gorge the river flows through a narrow crack in the lava.

Successful or not, it's always a pleasure just to be on the Rogue.

For ten million years, the land was relatively quiet. Then a new eruptive phase began about seven million years ago. This time the earth spewed andesite, a rock that didn't flow as easily as the earlier emissions. The andesite piled up around the vents, creating high peaks such as Mt. Hood, the Three Sisters, and Mt. McLoughlin. These new mountains rested on top of and somewhat to the east of the old Western Cascades. When this last eruptive phase began, the upper Rogue River flowed through a canyon almost 700 feet deep. The creation of the new mountains filled this canyon and pushed the river westward until it ran along the junction of the Western Cascades and the new High Cascades.

The Rogue began on the slopes of one of the new mountains, a 12,000-foot peak called Mt. Mazama. As the ice ages came and went (and may come again), the Rogue Country supported a changing array of fish and wildlife. Salmon and steelhead nosed in from the sea, then shouldered their way through powerful rapids; survivors spawned in the river, no doubt dodging the huge feet of the mammoths and mastodons that had waded in for a drink.

About 6,800 years ago, Mt. Mazama began a series of violent eruptions that spewed 13 cubic miles of volcanic material over much of western North America. An ash blanket spread as far east as Saskatchewan, and Mazama's lower slopes were covered by as much as 300 feet of red-hot pumice. Mazama blew out so much of its innards that its walls no longer had internal support. The upper half of the mountain caved in, creating an immense crater that filled with water. Today it is one of the most beautiful places in Oregon: Crater Lake.

The Mazama cataclysm buried the Upper Rogue. Deprived of its channel, the upper river meandered. Due to the porous nature of the pumice, much of it actually flowed underground. In time, the upper river unearthed itself and found its present streambed; in geologic terms, it's a very recent channel. This new-ish river linked up with the old Rogue that had flowed through the Klamaths for millions of years.

Mazama's eruptions were not unwitnessed by humans. Before and after the mountain's eruptions, people had been coming and going in the Rogue Country for millennia. About 2,000 years ago, an Athabascan-speaking group related to the Apache and Navaho settled near the mouth of the Rogue. They lived in communal cedar-plank houses in permanent settlements of 30 to 150 people. These coastal bands are often lumped together and referred to as "Tututni." They were not a "tribe," in the political sense, but the bands had similar cultures.

A placid section of the Wild Rogue Canyon.

Upriver, bands of Kalapuyan-speakers (Takelmas) settled in the Rogue Valley and lived in similar dwellings built from sugar pine. Their culture was much like that of the coastal bands.

It's estimated that at the time of European contact, there were 10,000 Indians in the Rogue Country, most of whom dwelt near the river's mouth. They lived a simple life centered around the sea and the river, the fish and the game, and the rituals and traditions that bound them together.

Much of the Indian culture focused on salmon. They burned the hills near the entrance to the Rogue, believing this would bring more fish into the river. Salmon were always split up the backbone with a stone knife, and it was taboo for a youth's immediate family to eat his first salmon. If you spoke of land animals or women when you were fishing at sea, your companions would throw you overboard—permanently.

In the river, they caught salmon in dip nets fashioned from vine maple hoops covered with woven mesh, and sometimes with spears. When salmon were less plentiful, they used hooks made from bone and fished in the river's deep pools. Smelt, shellfish, camas bulbs, acorns, and grass seed were other staples of the Indian diet. Life for them was not easy, but if they followed their rituals and traditions and worked hard, they could survive.

The Spanish were the first Europeans to sail along the Pacific coast. Later, fur traders made direct contact with the Indians, bartering beads and iron goods for the pelts of beaver and sea

Osprey are a common sight along the river.

otter. In the late 18th century, the Indians of the Rogue Country approached the whites with openness and curiosity. Within 30 years, however, they were extremely wary and cautious of all

A wild October steelhead poses before being released. Most fly anglers release their steelhead.

Black Bar Lodge on the Wild Rogue section is a pleasant haven for river drifters.

whites; one can only speculate on the experiences that changed their attitude.

When Jedidiah Smith came through the area in 1828, Indians attacked his party, killing 14 men. Smith and three others escaped.

September and October are fly-fishing-only months on the upper Rogue.

(Smith has two steelhead rivers named for him: one in Northern California and one in Oregon). Bands of Indians continued to fire arrows at the occasional groups of whites that traveled the crude road between Oregon and California. Because of the attacks, the whites named the Indians "Rogues," and the river along which they lived was called the Rogue's River.

Given time, a peaceful solution to the Indian conflicts might have been found. Instead, events of past eons created a holocaust that left many corpses, most of them Indian. The crux of the problem lay in the islands that collided with the coast 250 million years before. They were rich in minerals: copper, nickel, chromite . . . and gold. No doubt the Indians had noticed the glittering flecks in the river—you can still see them today—but they had no use for them. To the Indians, wealth meant owning a canoe, or dentalium shells, or the bright red scalp of a pileated woodpecker. The idea of white people flocking to the Rogue Country in search of the yellow metal was inconceivable. But gold-fever doomed the Indians and their fish-centered lives.

In 1852, packers trailing a lost mule found gold near Table Rock on the Upper Rogue. Not long after, a single 15-foot vein was found near the town of Gold Hill; it yielded $700,000. The discoveries brought thousands of gold-seekers up from California and down from the farms of the Willamette Valley. For awhile, Jackson County, in the heart of the Rogue Country, was the most populous county in Oregon.

The miners are often described as a "rough bunch." The description seems inadequate. Some of the miners were decent men, but many more were the greedheads, malcontents, and drunken rabble that gravitate to a lawless society. They had a simple solution for dealing with the vexatious Indian bands: exterminate every man, woman, and child.

Acting on pretexts as slight as an Indian riding a horse without permission, they attacked isolated Indians and sleeping villages. They killed indiscriminately, without regard to age or sex. In 1853, a family of settlers arrived in Jacksonville with a seven-year-old Indian boy in their care. The town's miners saw the child and cried "hang him, hang him." Cooler heads almost prevailed, but a man rode into town screaming, "Exterminate the whole race. We have been in the Valley killing Indians all day." A few minutes later, they had a rope around the lad's neck and strung him up.

Unfortunately, this was not a unique event. Despite treaties and occasional peace, a familiar pattern developed: miners would slaughter the women, children, and old men of a peaceful Indian village. Indian warriors would then attack a few isolated white miners and settlers who probably were not involved in the massacre. This would bring more slaughter of Indians, most of whom had nothing to do with the attacks on the whites. It was a war in which most of the victims were innocent.

A heron contemplates a fishing hole of its own.

In 1855, Indians responded to the massacres and swept through the Rogue Valley, attacking settlers and miners. They holed up in the Rogue canyon where rugged terrain made them

Ledges, pocket water, troughs, and slots near the bank provide the best steelhead fishing.

*One of Zane Grey's river boats is stored
near his cabin at Winkle Bar.*

Some of the new settlers realized the Rogue Country's real bonanza was its fish. In the 1870s, a cannery was set up near the mouth of the river; it pioneered canning technology that later moved north to the Columbia River. Most of the area's new inhabitants were pragmatic about the Rogue's fish, viewing them as cheap meat and a source of income. One settler, a hermit known as Old Man Ramey, made his living by gaffing salmon that stacked up at a falls in the canyon; his name was corrupted to "Rainie," and those falls now bear his name.

Most of the early commercial fishing took place at the river's mouth and around Grants Pass, with many salmon taken in gillnets. At the same time, sport anglers had discovered the Rogue, doing most of their fishing near Shady Cove on the upper river.

Conflicts between sport and commercial interests arose, and in 1910 the Rogue River Fish Protection Association was formed to combat declining steelhead runs. This group gathered 11,000 signatures to put a measure on the state ballot that would close the Rogue to all fishing but that done with hook and line. The Grants Pass gillnetters claimed that most of the signers were from Portland and shouldn't have any say in "their" river. Voters passed the measure, but three years later the legislature overturned the people's will in favor of commercial interests.

One reason there was so much gillnetting at Grants Pass was because salmon stacked up behind Ament Dam. Ament Dam had poor fish passage and was a known salmon and steelhead killer. Because of its obvious problems, many people sought to have Ament Dam dismantled, but a small number of local vested interests put up strong resistance. Eventually it was removed, and a new structure was put in upriver from it: Savage Rapids Dam. Savage Rapids Dam has poor fish passage and is a known salmon and steelhead killer. Because of its obvious problems, many people have sought to have Savage Rapids Dam dismantled, but a small number of local vested interests have put up strong resistance. This dam still stands.

The more things change, the more they stay the same.

One of the earliest anglers to publicize the Rogue River was Zane Grey, the famous writer of western novels. He began visiting the Rogue in 1919, and in 1928 he built a small log cabin at Winkle Bar in the Wild Rogue section. For the next seven years, he visited both the Rogue and the North Umpqua rivers, and wrote extensively about the Rogue in his book *Tales of Freshwater Fishing.*

A mass of fungi grows beside the river.

difficult to dislodge. Eventually, they agreed to settle on a reservation to the north, where miners couldn't get at them. But even as Indians traveled down the Rogue in canoes, headed for government protection at the coast, they were attacked. Canoes were upset in the treacherous rapids, and many Indians drowned.

When the rocky islands collided with the continent, they were assimilated and became a part of it. The collision of white and Indian cultures had a different result: to escape persecution, the Indian survivors settled on a reservation near the Willamette Valley, and their cultural presence disappeared from the region.

River Rats and Movie Stars

Mining devastated more than the Indian culture. It almost destroyed the river's fish, as well. Entire spawning creeks were re-routed to run sluice boxes. Dredging and hydraulic mining filled the river with silt and greatly depressed fish reproduction.

In a few years, the easy gold was taken out. There were no new finds, so most of the miners left in search of the next strike. The Rogue Valley began to fill with farmers and families. The river flushed out the debris of mining, and the fish replenished themselves, just as they had done after the region's natural cataclysms.

An early morning angler waits for a grab on the upper Rogue.

You can still find people in the area that remember Grey. They have a consistent opinion of him: he was a vain, conceited, arrogant, bigoted, miserly, totally self-centered son-of-a-bitch. Still, he was a dedicated angler with a strong sense of conservation. He believed that Oregonians failed to recognize the value of their great fisheries and might destroy them in a rush of short-sighted economic development.

Zane Grey's cabin still stands and is visited by anglers and river drifters. The property was owned for many years by Walter Haas, who until his recent death was chairman of Levi Strauss, the clothing company. Those who knew him say Haas was as generous and self-effacing as Grey was stingy and egotistical.

The Rogue became a popular river for other celebrities. In 1940, movie queen Ginger Rogers bought an 1,800-acre ranch on the Upper Rogue, downstream from Shady Cove. *Life* magazine once featured Rogers on its cover. She was clad in a very un-sexy pair of waders and was holding a fly rod. It was not just a studio pose; Ginger was an ardent and accomplished fly angler.

A man who guided her on the Rogue said of her: "One of the best guests we ever had on a trip was Ginger Rogers. She didn't hesitate to wash dishes or do any other thing that needed to be done around camp."

The river guide who made that statement was Glenn Wooldridge, a Grants Pass native and self-acknowledged "river rat." In 1915, when he was 19 years old, Wooldridge wanted to make a trip down the Rogue to the coast, something few people had done since the Indians ruled the river. He and a friend built a 20-foot boat from cedar planks and 2x4s and floated to Gold Beach. Many of the rapids had to be portaged around, including Blossom Bar. At that time, Blossom Bar was a huge rock garden with no passage. Wooldridge had to drag the heavy boat over the rocks for half a day just to get through.

Wooldridge became a river guide and boat builder. He shepherded "dudes" around Shady Cove through the summer, then took them on 10-day trips through the Wild Rogue canyon in the fall. Hauling gear and boats over Blossom Bar's rocks got tiresome, so Wooldridge and others (with government permission) dynamited a passage through the rocks. He blasted rocks from other major rapids, as well.

Wooldridge retired from guiding in 1955, but continued to build boats into his 80s, switching from cedar planks to plywood

Inside Zane Grey's cabin at Winkle Bar.

to aluminum. After World War II, he started using motors, and in 1947 made the first upriver trip from Gold Beach to Grants Pass. Ever the river rat and adventurer, he became the first person to run the Hells Gate Canyon on Canada's Fraser River—when he was 79 years old. Wooldridge's grandsons still build river boats.

A Fish for Every Season

There isn't a month when fresh anadromous fish don't enter the Rogue River. It is one of the Northwest's richest streams, supporting large numbers of spring and fall chinook salmon, coho salmon, summer and winter steelhead, trout and other fish. The river's two main tributaries, the Applegate and Illinois rivers, support wild strains of anadromous fish that use the Rogue as a "freeway" before finding the right offramp for their home waters.

Many of the fish are wild and spawn in the river's mainstem. They enrich the Rogue in several ways: by digging spawning redds that refresh the river's gravel; by providing spawn that feeds other fish and aquatic life; and by leaving a carcass that releases nutrients to the river.

Seven kinds of fish are eagerly pursued by Rogue anglers. They are briefly described as follows.

Half-Pounders. "Half-pounders" are unique to the Rogue, Klamath, and Eel rivers. They are "boomerang" steelhead, homebody fish that don't wander far from their natal rivers. Like most steelhead, half-pounders smolt when they are about seven inches long and head for the ocean, usually between March and May. But instead of waiting two or three years before they return, the half-pounders come back to the Rogue the next fall, even though they are not yet sexually mature. Some may stay in the river another year, feeding like trout, before heading out again. Others return to the ocean in spring. And the next fall, they're back as mature steelhead.

The typical half-pounder is 12 to 16 inches long (and often weighs more than half a pound). When they first return in the fall, they are aggressive and readily take a fly. After a few weeks in the river, they feed like trout again and can provide good fishing when pursued with winter fly-fishing techniques. Most half-pounders only return as far as the Wild Rogue section, although you can find a few as far up as Shady Cove. About 95% of the Rogue basin's summer steelhead have a half-pounder life history. About half of the winter steelhead bound for the Rogue and its Applegate tributary also have a half-pounder history, but none of the winter fish headed for the Illinois River (another major tributary) were half-pounders.

Summer Steelhead. The typical Rogue summer steelhead is between 18 and 22 inches long—about three pounds on average. This relatively small size is due to the half-pounder life history: less time in the ocean means less time growing big off its rich feeding grounds. Today, about half the summer steelhead are wild, and the hatchery fish are descended from native Rogue steelhead.

Summer fish enter the Rogue beginning in May, and can move upstream quickly. By July, there can be good steelheading in the Upper Rogue. Over the last ten years, the run has averaged more than 12,000 fish above Gold Ray Dam, with the bulk showing up in September and October. These months can offer superb fishing: sunny skies, fall colors, and bountiful fish. Summer steelhead spread throughout the Rogue system (except the Illinois River). Although most fish are in the two- to four-pound range, there are enough over five pounds—and a few over ten—to keep anglers on their toes.

The Rogue's summer steelhead spawn between December and March. In a reversal of "normal" steelhead behavior, many summer steelhead dig their redds in the tributaries, then their fry migrate to the mainstem for rearing. In yet another deviation from the norm, the Rogue's summer-run steelhead continue to feed after returning to the river. Hatchery fish (the only ones that can be killed) often have stomachs full of stonefly nymphs, caddis pupae, and salmon eggs. This feeding behavior affects the tactics for catching the fish; more on that later.

Winter Steelhead. Winter fish enter the Rogue beginning in November. Fresh fish arrive December through March, and they

Most Rogue River steelhead weigh three or four pounds, but some—like this one—grow to six or seven.

Martin James, a visitor from England, holds his first Rogue steelhead.

spread throughout the river. Bright winter fish can even be found in April. The winter run is almost as large as the summer run.

Over 80% of the Rogue's winter steelhead are wild fish. They spawn as early as December and as late as June, but the heaviest spawning is in March and April. Unlike the summer fish, they spawn in the mainstem. Winter steelhead tend to be larger than their summer-run cousins, partly because only 50% of them have a half-pounder life history.

Spring Chinook Salmon. The Rogue supports a major run of spring chinook salmon. Most "springers" spend three years in the ocean, then begin their upriver journey between March and June. Runs vary between 10,000 and 80,000 fish. These salmon are typically 12 to 18 pounds, although there are larger ones, especially those that are wild.

When Lost Creek Dam was built in 1978, it blocked access to the Rogue's major spring salmon spawning habitat. As "mitigation" (can the loss of natural spawning habitat ever be truly mitigated?), a large hatchery was built at the base of the dam, and 80% of the run now comes from stocked fish. Still, 20% of the chinook are wild, so beginning in September there are thousands of wild salmon spawning in the Rogue's mainstem.

As is typical with spring chinook, these fish are still bright several months after entering the river, but they slowly darken and lose their strength. By August you might hook one while fishing for steelhead, but by then they lack the energy to be strong fighters. When you know you've hooked one, break it off rather than stressing it.

Wild turkeys are not uncommon in the Wild Rogue Canyon.

Fall Chinook Salmon. Nearly all the Rogue's fall chinook are wild. Most are slightly larger than the springers due to the extra time in the ocean, and some are truly huge—forty, fifty, even sixty pounds. They enter the estuaries in July, and by August many are in the Grants Pass area. There are two distinct runs. The first comes early—August or even July—and is destined for the Middle Rogue and Applegate River; 40,000 fish or more can be in this run. A later-running strain is bound for the Illinois River. Spawning begins in early October. They turn dark soon after entering the river, but sometimes you can spot a bright fish and cast to it. And if it takes your fly, your tackle will be tested to its limits.

Coho Salmon. Coho salmon are smaller than their chinook cousins, weighing only six or seven pounds. They are fine fly-fishing fare. Unlike chinook, which rely on weight and brute strength, coho are hard-running fish that tend to jump. They head upriver beginning in September and October, and provide good sport through November. By late November, they are well-distributed throughout the Rogue and begin spawning. The run is about evenly split between hatchery and wild fish.

Trout. Both rainbow and cutthroat trout are present in the Rogue, and there are even a few brown trout and brook trout above Lost Creek Dam. The Oregon Department of Fish and Wildlife puts juvenile hatchery fish in the "Holy Water" stretch below Lost Creek Dam, but the rest of the river is not stocked.

Trout are stocked in the lakes, however, and it is believed that some of them have either migrated or "leaked" into the river. Other rainbows are steelhead that lost the urge to migrate, and some are from ancient strains that persist in the headwater creeks. Cutthroat trout are present and tend to occupy slack-water pools with overhead cover. I've heard stories of four-pound cutts taken on flies; I've never seen one that big, but the tale-tellers seem like honest folk.

Other Fish. There is a significant run of shad that comes up the river in late spring. They reach as high as Rainie Falls. Few people fish for them, however. Both largemouth and smallmouth bass are present in Lost Creek and Applegate Reservoirs; a few leak into the rivers and provide a surprise to unsuspecting anglers.

Dennis Becklin, a Grants Pass angler and businessman, recently analyzed almost 60 years of streamflow and fish count information. He reached some significant conclusions about the relationship between streamflow and the health of the Rogue's anadromous fish runs. In brief, Dennis's analysis shows that the long-term spring chinook salmon population is directly related to total flow in the river basin; in other words, springers do best when flows are higher than average. On the other hand, the coho salmon population is inversely related to river flow; they do best when flows are moderate to low. Summer steelhead respond to river flows in much the same manner as coho, but

The "Holy Water" is a fly-only section with well-fed rainbow trout.

The author holds a bright winter-run steelhead taken with an indicator rig on the Applegate, a Rogue tributary.

are not as affected by higher flows. Winter steelhead seem to be the most adaptable to changes in river flow; short of major floods their population is stable. Fall chinook are highly dependent on releases from Lost Creek Dam, and with careful control of flows their population has skyrocketed.

Further, Dennis's analysis shows that major floods resulted in a short-term loss of fish (the results show up three years after the flood), but in the long term the fish rebound strongly after a flood refreshes the river's spawning gravel. There was a major flood in early 1996, and an even bigger one on New Year's Day 1997. These events will probably have a big impact—first negative, then positive—on the Rogue's anadromous fish population in 1999 and 2000.

Flies

With so many kinds of fish to be caught, and under so many different conditions, a well-rounded Rogue angler needs a versatile fly box. The fly plates show a few of the most effective patterns for steelhead, salmon, trout, and half-pounders.

As mentioned in the section on Steelhead Tactics, traditional patterns and presentations are not always the best way to catch the Rogue's steelhead. One of the most effective flies in recent years is the Big Bird. This fly was originated by Mike St. John, one of the best guides on the Upper Rogue. It doesn't look like much until you think about it a bit. It's really a bead-headed Hare's Ear Soft Hackle. When fished below an indicator, it gets down quick and looks "buggy," suggestive of a caddis pupa in fall or a March brown in winter. Look at this fly and the Tiger

Paw, which is one of the best half-pounder patterns. Compared to many steelhead patterns, both are a tad drab, and I think drabness is often a key to good Rogue patterns.

An arsenal of flies for spring chinook salmon.

Trout Flies (by Dave Roberts)

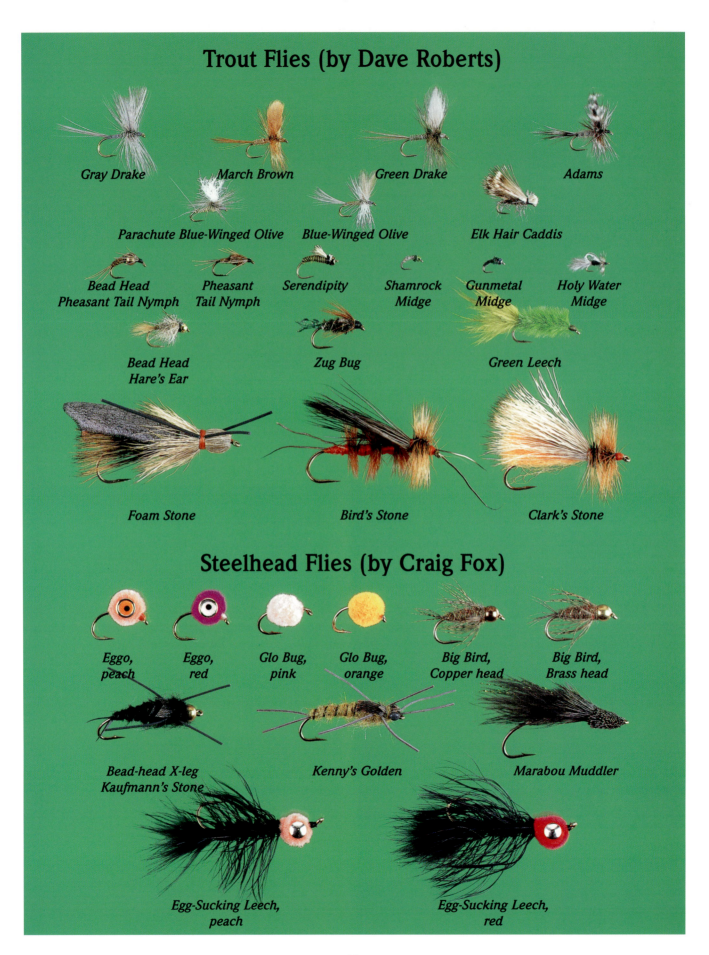

Gray Drake

March Brown

Green Drake

Adams

Parachute Blue-Winged Olive

Blue-Winged Olive

Elk Hair Caddis

Bead Head
Pheasant Tail Nymph

Pheasant
Tail Nymph

Serendipity

Shamrock
Midge

Gunmetal
Midge

Holy Water
Midge

Bead Head
Hare's Ear

Zug Bug

Green Leech

Foam Stone

Bird's Stone

Clark's Stone

Steelhead Flies (by Craig Fox)

Eggo,
peach

Eggo,
red

Glo Bug,
pink

Glo Bug,
orange

Big Bird,
Copper head

Big Bird,
Brass head

Bead-head X-leg
Kaufmann's Stone

Kenny's Golden

Marabou Muddler

Egg-Sucking Leech,
peach

Egg-Sucking Leech,
red

Half-Pounder Flies (by Craig Fox)

Brindlebug

Red Ant

Tiger Paw

Green Butt Skunk

Silver Hilton

Street Walker

Salmon Flies (by Ron Tenison)

Chartreuse Bunny Leech

Chartreuse-Legs Girdlebug

Chartreuse Flash

Hairy Butt

Fall Demon

Red Bouncer

Spring Trailer

Egg patterns are very effective in fall and winter because there is so much spawn in the river. The Eggo pattern is a Glo Bug with nickel eyes to get it down to the bottom. Many tiers put the stick-on eyes on the barbell—not to suggest an egg with eyeballs, but to tone down the brightness of the barbell.

Master fly-tier Dave Roberts says he once saw a stonefly in the upper river with a salmon egg in its mouth—and a steelhead zipped across and ate it. So maybe the infamous Egg Sucking Leech looks like something natural after all.

Most of the salmon flies are patterns developed by Ron Tenison. They are used as follows.

Chartreuse Flash: Spring chinook. The ball at the end gives it a lot of "wiggle" in the water.

Chartreuse Bunny Leech: Spring chinook.

Chartreuse-Legs Girdlebug: Spring chinook.

Spring Trailer: Spring chinook. Use it as a trailing fly behind a large fly such as the Girdlebug

Red Bouncer: Spring chinook. Use it in riffles.

Fall Demon: Fall chinook.

Hairy Butt: Coho.

Fall Demon: Fall chinook.

Steelhead Tactics

Summer steelhead begin nosing their way into the Rogue in May, and fresh fish will continue to enter right through December, with a peak in September and October. The first winter steelhead swim upriver alongside the last of the summer fish, and even in April you can find mint-bright winter steelhead. So there is hardly a time of year when you can't find fresh steelhead somewhere in the Rogue. (During September and October, the regulations don't allow lead on the leader in the Upper Rogue.)

As you might expect, water temperature, river level, and other factors vary greatly throughout the year. Good Rogue fly anglers know several tactics that work well, and will choose the ones that best fit conditions on the day they are fishing. I'll only mention the most productive techniques.

Classic Wet-Fly Swing. The traditional cast-swing-step technique has its place here, especially for summer steelhead. A seven-weight rod is the most versatile; an eight-weight is a bit

Big Bird fly with a yarn indicator—deadly fall tactics for steelhead.

Looking for a silver strike amid autumn's gold.

heavy for most summer fish, and a six-weight will be too little for the occasional ten-pounder. Use a floating line with a nine-foot leader tapered to 1X; either a weight-forward fly line or a double taper will work, but the double taper will do better when you have the brush at your back and need to roll cast. Use a traditional steelhead fly, such as a Green Butt Skunk or a Street Walker.

Look for water that is three to six feet deep with the current moving at the speed of a walk. Underwater structures, such as rocks and ledges, can be important, but are not essential. You will often find this kind of water downstream from a point of land or a pile of boulders. Steelhead will be lying in the transition zone as the current changes from fast to slow (but not in stagnant water). You should be able to reach the run by casting from shore, not from a boat. If there is a backeddy near shore, or if there is a sudden break between fast water and slow, seek a new run.

Cast across river at about a 45-degree angle. Immediately mend line (usually upstream) so the fly will slowly cross the river with your fly line as straight as you can get it. Lead the fly slightly with the rod. Then do nothing—don't wiggle the rod, mend line or strip line—until the fly has stopped below you. When your fly reaches the end of its swing, step downstream about three feet and cast again. Cast-swing-step your way downstream until you've covered all the water in the run.

When your fly passes over a willing steelhead, the fish will follow your fly, then (maybe) take the fly in its mouth and begin to return to its lie, thus pulling the hook into the corner of its jaw. When you first feel the line tighten, swing your rod to shore. Don't strike! Let the fish hook itself; if you strike hard and fast you risk ripping the fly out of the fish's mouth.

Once a steelhead is hooked, hold your rod more to the side rather than vertically. This keeps side pressure on the fish so it can't get its head into the current, thus making it work harder and tire more quickly.

Often, steelhead will pluck at a fly without getting hooked, and sometimes they will boil behind it without touching it.

A winter angler carefully places his fly so it will drift through a slot of holding water.

Most of these fish can be brought back to the fly, so when you feel a strong pluck but don't hook a fish, cast again (immediately). If you still have no hookup, walk back upstream about five feet and resume your cast-step-cast through the run.

Deep Drift. While the Rogue offers many runs and conditions where a classic wet-fly swing is appropriate, there are many more times and places that call for a different approach. On the Rogue, some of the best steelhead spots are pocket water behind boulders, slots in midriver or near the bank, along ledges, and sudden transitions from shallow to deep water. This is especially true on the Upper Rogue.

Also, water temperature can be quite low; even in September and October, the water can be 45 degrees or less. At that temperature, a steelhead's metabolism is slowed so that it is likely to hold near the bottom and not move far for a fly. In addition, many salmon spawn in the upper and middle sections of the Rogue, and the steelhead feed on the spawn. Summer fish also actively feed on stonefly nymphs and caddis pupae in September and October.

These conditions dictate different tactics than the traditional wet-fly swing. The fly must be presented near the bottom and should imitate the behavior and appearance of the natural food.

One way of getting down to the fish is to use a heavy sink-tip line and a traditional fly. The tactics are essentially the same as the classic approach described above, but the sink-tip carries the fly deeper and (with luck) reaches the fish.

Another approach is less conventional but works far better. Use a seven- or eight-weight rod and a floating line with five to seven feet of leader tapered to 1X. Take two inches of thick poly yarn and comb it out so the strands are mostly separated, then

For those who look there is splendor in the grass.

fasten it the leader with an improved clinch knot around the middle. Dress the yarn heavily with fly floatant. Just above the yarn indicator, tie a length of 2X or 3X tippet directly to the 1X leader with a clinch knot; ideally, this leader should be about six inches longer than the depth of the water.

In this system, the yarn serves as an indicator and keeps the fly at a consistent depth. The right angle joint between the two leader sections helps the fly sink more quickly and drift more naturally. The thin tippet helps get the fly down, too.

Tie on a fly that matches the prevailing food the steelhead are feeding on; current regulations allow up to three flies, although most anglers find this rig hard enough to cast with only one or two flies. If the salmon are on their redds, use an egg pattern. If steelhead are actively feeding on caddis pupae, use a caddis imitation such as the Big Bird. You can recognize this latter feeding situation because you will see a few steelhead porpoise on the surface, just like feeding trout. Don't be lead astray, however; you will catch more fish by drifting your fly deeply than by switching to a near-surface pattern. When your rig reaches the end of its drift, let it swing across in the current. This causes the fly to rise and sometimes triggers arm-wrenching strikes from steelhead.

When fishing this way, remember it takes awhile for the fly to sink to the right depth, so you have to cast upstream from where you think the steelhead are. If the salmon are on their redds, steelhead will gather below them and take their spawn, so cast your egg fly right on top of the salmon. The fly will sink to bottom downstream from them, which is where the steelhead will be waiting.

Even if steelhead are not feeding on salmon spawn or caddis pupae, this technique works well in pocket water and slots. It is especially suited to fishing from a drifting boat; you just cast to the side and downstream from the boat, then let both fly and boat drift naturally in the current.

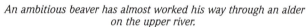
An ambitious beaver has almost worked his way through an alder on the upper river.

A worker at Cole M. Rivers hatchery clips the fin of a hatchery smolt so it can be distinguished from wild fish.

After your cast, stack-mend line behind the indicator. Then treat the indicator like a dry fly, mending line so it has a natural drift. Manage your loose line so you can strike quickly, and try to keep your fly line upstream from the indicator.

If the aesthetics of this technique bother you, keep in mind that it uses an imitation of natural food presented in a natural manner, and it is adapted to the environmental conditions in which the fish live. Also, it requires more skill to cast and to detect a strike than the classic steelheading techniques. Admittedly, it is not graceful. The yarn has so much

wind resistance that it's a pig to cast and requires an open-loop casting stroke, and the indicator/depth-adjuster looks like a powder puff floating down the river. And this style of fishing is more intense because you spend all day staring at your indicator instead of looking around at the birds and trees.

If trout fishing with big stonefly nymphs and an indicator bothers you, then you probably won't like this tactic either and should stick to a classic approach. Of course, when steelhead are most plentiful, you won't have as much action as the dead-drifters. And you'll have to endure their whoops and hollers as they come down the river behind you and pick up the steelhead you missed.

Winter Steelheading. There are as many steelhead coming up the Rogue in winter as in fall. February through April, fishing in the Upper Rogue can be excellent, and not many people take advantage of it. The techniques are basically the same as in the fall, but you have to deal with more high water and fluctuating river levels. Dead drifted egg patterns will produce well through April. Another effective tactic is casting a lead-eye leech into pocket water and chutes. Let it drift near the bottom or swing past rocky holding water.

Chinook Salmon Tactics

There was a time when anyone who pursued chinook salmon with a fly rod was regarded as a candidate for the loony bin. But thanks to modern tackle and tactics, it's no longer such a nutty

End of the journey: Stripped of eggs and milt, hatchery-reared chinook salmon await their final destiny.

In springtime, fly anglers need to be careful of migrating salmon and steelhead smolts. If you're catching smolts, move to a new spot.

option. Still, when you're hooked to a bright salmon, you may briefly wonder what you've gotten yourself into.

Ron Tenison has aggressively pursued salmon with a fly rod for over twenty years. He now lives near the Rogue and has studied its salmon carefully. Each spring, he conducts a clinic at McKenzie Outfitters in Medford.

"Spring fish are my favorite," Ron says. "They're the most active and usually weigh between 18 and 25 pounds. I prefer the male fish, even though they're smaller than the hens. The males are more aggressive and more spectacular fighters. The fall fish are bigger—my personal best weighed 69 pounds—but they just wear you down. The male springers are more fun."

For spring chinook salmon—referred to as *springers*—Ron recommends a good 10-weight rod and a disk-drag reel with 300 yards of backing. Terminal tackle and tactics depend on the type of water you're fishing, which in turn depends on the season and the time of day.

In the morning (dawn to 10 a.m.), springers are usually in riffles 4-6 feet deep, with a broken surface over cobbles and other structure. By midday (10 a.m. to 4 p.m.), moving water over deep holes is the best place to look for them; the water is usually 10-12 feet deep, but it is *not* stagnant. By evening (4 p.m. to dark), tailouts are good places; fish move into them about an hour before dark. This latter water is Ron's favorite; he knows over 30 such runs in the Upper and Middle Rogue, all of them suitable for fly fishing and reachable without a boat.

When fishing the riffles, Ron recommends a floating line (you'll have better control with a double taper) and a weighted leader at least nine-feet long, plus a three-foot tippet with 12-15 pound breaking strength. The tippet needs to be long so the fly will float up and not snag fish (or bottom). Don't use too strong a tippet. Seriously, some of these fish you just don't want to be connected to, so you need something you can break.

Big flies such as black Matukas or rabbit leeches in black, blue, or chartreuse are good. Sometimes a smaller trailer fly of chartreuse crystalflash works well; the male salmon are attracted by the big fly, then take the small one. Cast the fly upstream so it will sink, then let it swing around. At the end of the swing,

strip three times, pulling in two feet with each strip. Then let the fly drop back two feet. Repeat the strip-drop technique until all the line is in; sometimes salmon will follow it and take the fly right at your feet.

In the tailouts, use a sink-tip line. You *must* have control of the fly line, so don't use a tip longer or shorter than ten feet. The leader should be unweighted with seven feet of taper plus a three-foot tippet of 12-pound breaking strength. Tie on a single fly, such as a size 6 to 10 Comet-style pattern with all maribou (fluorescent red plus chartreuse is good). Use the same presentation described above for riffles.

When a fresh spring chinook hits your fly, it will explode. It's not unusual for a fish to run 150 feet in just a few seconds, then jump four feet in the air, then run again. As you might expect, you need a high-quality reel to handle fish like this. A good disk drag is essential. Ron Tenison actually recommends pointing the rod straight at the salmon when they are on a tear. "If you've put a deep bend in your rod," he says, "then the fish jumps, the line will bounce back and likely wrap around the tip of your rod. Then the fish makes another run, and it's bye-bye fly rod. I've seen it happen too many times. Just point the rod at the fish and let the reel take it."

Chinook prefer to travel under low light. Anglers can take advantage of this habit at dawn and dusk by positioning themselves where the structure of the river constrains the salmon to

Two deer come to the river for a drink.

a narrow slot. These slots may be less than ten feet wide and six to eight feet deep. Cast so your fly drifts through the slot near the river bottom. The fact is, most traveling chinook will ignore you, but even if 95% of them just don't want to know about you and your silly fly, there are a lot of fish in the river, so your chances of finding a willing one aren't too bad.

Spring chinook spawn about a month before the fall chinook. It is not unusual for fresh fall salmon to move in behind spawning springers and—for whatever reason—swallow the eggs that are spilled. One strategy for picking off fall chinook is to cast egg patterns so they drift along the bottom behind spawning springers. This is also an excellent way to catch steelhead (see the previous section). However, even in water that is only three or four feet deep, it can take a surprising amount of effort to get your fly down to the bottom where the salmon are. Egg patterns must be heavily weighted, and lead on the leader is often needed. (Note that in September and October it is illegal to put lead on the leader in the Upper Rogue section.)

When fishing like this, try to spot the bright fall salmon, then cast to them. This will reduce the chances of snagging a dark spawner. If you tie into a spawner, break it off immediately. And stay out of the redds; don't crunch your future sport under your wading boots.

Chinook are easily spooked. Even if they don't leave when you come near them, they will grow wary and unlikely to take a fly. That's why chinook fishing is almost always best when you first arrive at a pool. After awhile, the fish get wise to you and either sidle off or ignore your offering.

An exception to this is when you're casting to traveling salmon at dawn and dusk. If many fish are moving through a narrow slot or into a tailout, fresh, unjaded salmon are going to see your fly. In this case, it is best to hold your ground and keep casting. On the other hand, if you don't see moving fish and you're casting to salmon that have seen more of your fly than they care to, move on and find fresh fish.

When fly fishing for chinook salmon, proper choice of water is critical. Learning where the best places are takes a lot of exploration and observation—and a lot of fishless days. But once places and techniques are mastered, fishing can be outstanding. An evening of hooking three or four big spring salmon can give you such an adrenaline rush that you may have trouble sleeping.

Chinook salmon are big fish, and they are determined to make their way upstream. If they are moving aggressively, such as at dawn or dusk, they may swim right past your feet. And if you wade and step near one, it may move off with a powerful thrust of its tail—and knock your legs out from under you. That's why it's best to shuffle your feet along the bottom when you wade.

I fished one evening in the Grants Pass area with Ron Tenison. He told me about an incident from earlier that week. Some rowdy gear fisherman had been at the pool for awhile, and had spent more time drinking beer than casting. One of them fell into the river near a big pod of spawning salmon. About three dozen spooked chinook, weighing twenty to forty pounds each, rushed downriver. Another (sober) angler was standing in two feet of water when these fish sped past her. They upended her like she'd stood in the way of the Green Bay Packers front line.

Spey rod in hands, a winter angler launches a cast on the Illinois River, a Rogue tributary.

Coho Salmon Tactics

November is coho time on the Rogue. These hard-running and acrobatic salmon distribute themselves throughout the river and provide excellent sport, especially above Graves Creek.

Good places to find coho are in riffles where the water drops off. They like to school up, and while most fish in the school aren't the least bit interested in you or your fly, there's usually a few that can be enticed. Coho are chasers and may aggressively pursue a moving fly. Often, the faster the fly, the better they like it.

One approach is to cast a long line, then feed more line into the drift so you have as much as 150 feet of line out. Let it swing across the current. This often attracts the attention of several coho; some will follow the fly but not (usually) take it. When your fly is below the fish, start stripping it in as fast as you can. Use two hands to strip, if you dare. One or two fish will break off from the group of followers and chase your fly. Keep stripping! Don't stop! Coho may take your fly within a rod's length from you.

Guides are a good investment for those new to the Rogue's ways. Mike St. John helps an angler find a steelhead.

As you might suspect, line control can be a significant problem with this tactic. If you put 150 feet of line in your drift, then strip like a demon until a salmon takes the fly just off your boots, you will have a big fish that's mad as hell and pulling against a big heap of fly line that's coiled God knows how. There are many possible outcomes to this situation. You don't want to know about most of them.

Trout Tactics

It was early June, the peak of the salmonfly season on the Holy Water. As the sun edged toward the horizon, anglers arrived and took up their positions. Two hours before sunset, fly casters lined both sides of the river. They were seldom more than a hundred feet apart, so once an angler had staked his turf, he couldn't move to fresh water.

Huge, gravid salmonflies landed on the river. Some raised a ruckus, fluttering their four wings and sending ripples across the water. Others lay quietly, with wings folded across the back of their orange abdomen. And many disappeared into the mouths of eager trout.

The trout had been rising bank-to-bank since before most of the anglers arrived, but as each fisherman began casting, the rises soon stopped everywhere but in the middle of the river. Still, all the anglers kept casting. That is, all the anglers but one, a young man who sat on a rock near the shore.

This early morning steelhead grabbed a Green Butt Skunk on a swing—which is NOT how most Rogue steelhead are caught.

After ten or fifteen minutes, a trout rose to a salmonfly that drifted forty feet from the seated angler. Then another trout rose, downstream but only twenty feet from the bank. The angler approached the water in a crouch, knelt at the edge, and waited until he saw the flash of another rise. Then he cast ten

An angler's rod bends deep with the pull of a late-fall steelhead.

feet above where the trout had risen, using a reach cast so he would have a drag-free drift and little need to mend.

His Madam X fly floated to the trout's lie, a nose poked up, and the fly was sucked under. The angler played the fish from his kneeling position, and five minutes later he worked the fly out of the mouth of a well-conditioned 18-inch rainbow. Then the angler went back to his rock and sat some more, waiting for the rises to begin again.

At the end of the evening, this angler had spent only a third as much time casting as any other fisherman on the riverbank. But he'd caught the most fish.

Trout fishing on the Rogue is concentrated in the fly-only, catch-and-release Holy Water section. Here, trout do not compete with anadromous fish and are free to grow to large size. Although the geography is limited, the fishing can be excellent. But it can also be crowded, especially at popular times of year such as during the salmonfly hatch.

When the riverbank is chock-a-block with anglers, the best tool in your arsenal is patience. Don't keep casting, casting, casting. Take a break. Stake out your water, but spend more time sitting and watching than fishing. The river is full of trout, but if your line keeps drifting over their heads, they cease rising. Give them a break, and they will soon be feeding again. After you've hooked one, let the water rest before casting again. In the end, patience will catch more fish than brilliant casting or miracle fly patterns.

These trout have been educated by a lot of fly fishers, and it doesn't take much to put them down. Cast carefully, so the fly reaches the fish before the line and leader. Avoid wading. Approach stealthily, preferably on your knees. Cast short before casting long; the water deepens quickly, so many trout will be close to shore. And above all . . . patience.

Trout are seldom targeted by anglers in the rest of the river, and that's as it should be. There are so many salmon and steelhead smolts, and they can be such fools for a fly (with disastrous consequences for themselves), that they should just be left alone.

The Rogue has many of the standard Northwest hatches. November through April, blue-winged olives (*Baetis*) and midges dominate; use size 18 or 20 flies. A few March browns show up in March and early April. Caddis are prominent May through July, and again in September and October; size 16-18 Elk Hair dries work well in the Holy Water, but use size 14s on the mainstem. A few green drake duns can be found in late May. They overlap with the early appearance of salmonflies (adult *Pteronarcys californica* stoneflies). The salmonflies continue through June. June and July, the pale morning duns make an appearance on the mainstem but not in the Holy Water. Leech patterns can work well in July and August. A few gray drakes can be found in late October and early November.

A five- or six-weight rod with a floating line is the right tool. The water is clear and the current deceptively tricky, so 5X tippets are standard.

Half-Pounder Tactics

If you want to go after half-pounders, use a small fly (sizes 6 to 10) such as a Tiger Paw, and a five- or six-weight rod with a floating line. Present the fly with a traditional wet-fly swing. Floating lines work well in the morning, but when the light's on the water switch to a sinking line or sinking leader. Use a single

Dried thistles pick up the sun.

hook, play your fish quickly, never take them out of the water, and release them so they'll come back as mature steelhead.

Traditional Rogue half-pounder fly patterns such as the Juicy Bug used a double hook: a treble with one hook cut off. Don't do it; this style of fly tears up the fish too much. It belongs to an era when all fish were kept, and it has no place in catch-and-release fishing.

Some anglers twitch the rod tip as the fly swings. Half-pounders can be idiots when confronted with a twitched fly. Twitching works well from a boat. In the fall, you often see guides rowing their McKenzie boats against the current, with their clients twitching their rods every five seconds or so. It's a great way to keep non-flyfishing guides employed because they row just like they would if they were pulling plugs. And as in plug pulling, the client doesn't need to know diddly to catch fish—no casting, no presentation, the fish hooks itself. Occasionally you'll hear some guy say, "Yeah, I went to the Rogue last week and fly fished for the first time in my life. Caught 30 steelhead the first day." Technically this is a true statement, since half-pounders are steelhead, even if immature; but somehow it gives the wrong impression.

Oars straining, a rafter struggles to miss a rock in Blossom Bar Rapids.

After a few weeks in the river, half-pounders feed like trout. Throughout the winter, they can be caught by dead-drifting a small (size 18 or so) Pheasant Tail Nymph along the bottom, or on a dry blue-winged olive pattern when the hatch is on. By March, they will take March brown imitations; switch to a size 12 or 14 Pheasant Tail Nymph and a March brown Comparadun. The best places are drop-offs, along current seams, and just below riffles.

Half-pounders are especially thick in the Wild Rogue and Lower Rogue sections. The Agness and Illahee areas can have excellent summer and fall caddis hatches. Size 10 and 12 Brindle Bugs, or flies with olive and yellow bodies and rubber legs work well.

Boating the Rogue

It was a gorgeous, bright day in early fall. After prepping my drift boat, I climbed back into my truck. I shifted into reverse, ready to back down the ramp and head out for a pleasant afternoon and evening of fishing the Upper Rogue.

But before I could start moving, another rig pulled up next to mine and started down the ramp. "Jerk!" I muttered. "Wait your turn." In my mirror I could see his boat, a fancy yellow jet sled. I turned my head for a better view of this bad-mannered idiot with the expensive boat. Then I saw the writing on the boat's side: "Rescue." "Fire District #4." I pulled up out the way. Obviously something more important was happening than my fishing trip.

The jet sled splashed into the water, then roared upriver with several men aboard. As it disappeared around a bend, I spoke to one of the ground crew that had stayed behind. "Party of senior citizens," he said, and pointed at a tour bus in the parking lot. "They were headed downriver in several paddle

A group of rafters prepares for a spring float through the wild Rogue Canyon.

rafts piloted by a rafting contractor. Two boats flipped near the Obstinate J Ranch. Some of the folks are stranded on the other side of the river. We think they're all right, but we want to make sure." He gazed out over the river. "People have gotten careless. We've had ten years of drought, but now we're back to normal river flows. There's a lot more water then most folks are used to. They're too complacent. You've got to take this river seriously."

Half an hour later, I was able to launch my boat. All the seniors were found, and there were no casualties. Well, maybe one minor casualty: in a backeddy two miles downriver I found a white sunvisor with the name of the tour company on it.

Never take this river for granted. There are tricky currents and powerful hydraulics, and almost every section of the Rogue has places where you can get yourself into trouble. You should have at least intermediate whitewater skills to tackle any portion of the Rogue, and some sections, such as the Wild Rogue, require expert skills; Blossom Bar Rapids alone sinks about three dozen drift boats every year. Boaters who are used to easier, more forgiving rivers such as the Deschutes need to be alert and not overestimate their abilities.

Another word of caution: due to its ledgey, rocky nature, much of the Upper Rogue is tricky to anchor in. More than one boater has had his anchor drop between large boulders—never to be seen again.

The Illinois River is for experts only.

Headwaters

The river begins on the slopes of Mt. Mazama, the blown-out volcano whose deep caldera holds Crater Lake. At its beginnings, the Rogue is a mountain stream that sometimes meanders through grassy meadows, sometimes rushes through thick forests of Douglas fir. Except for the summer tourist crush, the river is often uncrowded and possesses some lovely campgrounds, a few of

A rescue boat heads out to retrieve rafters who capsized in a rapids. Those floating the river need good whitewater skills.

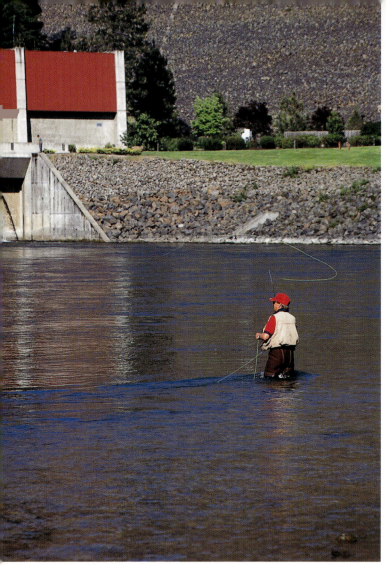

The "Holy Water" is a fly-only tailwater fishery below Lost Creek Dam.

We talked some about the fishing, and as his cigarette ash neared the filter, he nodded and said, "At least eight pounds, maybe nine." He ground the butt on a rock and dropped it into his wader pocket. "That was a deep fish," he said. "And thick. Definitely nine pounds."

By the time he drove home, I'm sure it was a ten-pounder.

The so-called "Holy Water" section of the Rogue is open year round for fly-fishing-only. It is a short stretch—barely half a mile long—between Lost Creek Dam and the salmon hatchery's diversion dam. Rainbow trout are stocked as fingerlings. Freed from competition from anadromous fish and protected from meat fishermen by catch-and-release regulations, they quickly grow large in the rich tailwater. Most, however, aren't as big as the six-seven-eight-nine-ten-pound rainbow mentioned above, and fall into the 15- to 20-inch range. But there are some really big ones out there.

This is a popular section of the river, especially during the salmonfly hatch of early June, when anglers are often only a cast apart. There is good access on both sides of the river. Most fishing takes place close to the dam, but good fish—and fewer anglers—can be found farther downstream. For the most part, the water is a flat run that moves at a moderate clip. It has sufficient depth to offer cover to the trout, but is not so deep you can't put a fly in front of them.

The town of Shady Cove is the center for fishing on the Upper Rogue. Fortunately, none of the river's fish look like the one on the sign!

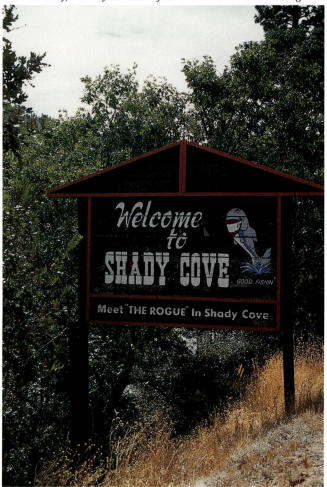

them far enough from the road to muffle traffic noise. Access is good from State Routes 62 and 230, and some areas have scenic trails alongside the river.

When Lost Creek Dam was built in 1978, it blocked the passage of salmon and steelhead into the headwaters of the Rogue, so the only fish in this section are trout. The Oregon Department of Fish and Wildlife believes the water is too cold to be productive, although other streams of similar temperature support good-sized trout. Regardless, this can be a pleasant place to cast a fly.

Holy Water

I heard a splash, followed by a whoop from the angler upstream from me. I turned in time to see a fat rainbow, easily two feet long, clear the water. A large orange fly hung from its jaw. After a ten-minute fight, the fish was at the beach and its captor asked me to snap some photos on his camera. I clicked the shutter a couple of times, then measured the trout against my rod: 26 inches. "About five pounds," I said. "Nice fish!" I eyed its girth and, feeling generous, added, "Maybe even six pounds."

"Oh yeah. Six pounds. Look at that belly," he said, his hands folded across his own gut. He reached down and worked the Clarks Stonefly from the fish's mouth. "Probably seven." The fish was released and swam off. "Seven for sure," he said as it disappeared. He sat on a rock and lit a cigarette. "Maybe eight."

The lazy days of summer on the Upper Rogue—shorts and T-shirt time.

To reach the Holy Water section, turn off State Route 62 where you see the signs for the Cole M. Rivers fish hatchery. For access to the east bank, turn right at the weir and follow the road to Rivers Edge Park. The dam is a short stroll from there. Rivers Edge Park is a pleasant, grassy spot, with ample parking, toilets, and picnic tables. Camping is not permitted.

To fish the west bank, bear left at the weir and park on the side of the road, opposite Rivers Edge Park. It's a quarter mile walk to the dam area. There is an outhouse toilet at the parking area.

The closest services to this section are in the town of Shady Cove in the Upper Rogue Section. There is camping at Rogue Elk Park (between the Holy Water and Shady Cove) and at Stewart State Park (farther up SR 62).

Upper Rogue

The Upper Rogue offers the finest steelhead fly fishing on the river. Its pockets, slots, breaks, and runs are ideal waters for enticing the sea-going rainbows to a well-presented fly.

This 28-mile-long stretch of the Rogue runs from the Holy Water to Gold Ray Dam. September and October, the regulations permit fly-fishing-only (but allow for a spinning rod with a bubble), and fall steelheading can be superb. A good guide can have several days a year when his two clients will hook over 20 mature steelhead between them. Of course, there are

also days when the count is zero; remember, we're talking about steelheading.

The river is frequently over 150 feet wide here. It has a rocky, sometimes ledgey structure with frequent stretches of shallow water and occasional very deep pools. Steelhead are often found in short pockets behind and in front of rocks, in

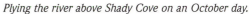

Plying the river above Shady Cove on an October day.

A hatchery-reared spring chinook salmon makes its final leap to end its journey at the Cole M. Rivers fish hatchery.

River access for bank anglers is adequate. Above Shady Cove, Highway 62 parallels the river, and there are public parks and roadside pullouts near good water. However, you are never far from road noise. Below Shady Cove, the highway leaves the river, and road noise fades away. Unfortunately for bank anglers, there is more private property below Shady Cove, so river access is lessened.

Boaters will find many launching and pull-out places along the Upper Rogue, but unless you have a jet boat, don't go below Tou Velle Park since that is the last take-out. There are some tricky rapids here, and beginning boaters may find this stretch—and most other sections of the Rogue—a little twitchy. Intermediate skills are recommended.

Above Shady Cove, there are several pullouts along the river; be respectful of private property and No Trespassing signs. Major public access points and facilities are:

Hatchery. Located just below the hatchery weir on the hatchery road. Gravel boat ramp with good parking; no other facilities. No fishing for a quarter mile downstream.

McGregor Park. Near the junction of SR 62 and the road to Rivers hatchery. Picnicking, toilets, children's play area; day-use only. Trails lead to the river.

Bridge Hole. Just downstream from McGregor Park. River access, porta-toilets, parking, picnic tables, a couple of BBQs. Day-use only.

slots near the bank, and below breaks. In other words, if you're used to riffle-run-tailout steelhead drifts—the sort of water suited to a traditional wet-fly swing—you'll need to revise your tactics. The structure of the river, low water temperatures in the fall, spawning salmon, and some unique habits of the fish, combine to dictate a different approach than that used on more classic waters such as the Deschutes (see the Steelhead Tactics section).

A drift boat picks its way through Blossom Bar, the river's most notorious rapids.

With a backdrop of snow-capped mountains and winter clouds, an angler fishes the upper Illinois River.

Casey State Park. On SR 62. Paved boat ramp, parking. Picnic tables, toilets; day-use only.
Rogue Elk County Park. On SR 62. Paved ramp, parking, picnicking, toilets, RV dump station. There are campsites (no RV hookups), but traffic on SR 62 is heavy, even at night; if road noise keeps you awake, try a little farther upstream at Stewart State Park.
Shady Cove Park. On Rogue River Dr. at its junction with SR 62. Paved ramp, parking, toilets, handicap platform, play area; day-use only.
Takelma County Park. Off Rogue River Dr. Primitive, Paved ramp, porta-toilets; day-use only.
Dodge Bridge. Off Rogue River Dr. at junction with SR 234. Paved ramp, handicap platform, toilets; day-use only.
Modoc. Brushy, litter-strewn, primitive area off Modoc Rd. It has several points of bank access and a crude, dirt boat ramp. Break-ins are frequent, so never let your car out of sight. Under no circumstances whatsoever should you even *think* about camping here.
Tou Velle State Park. Off Table Rock Rd. Pleasant picnic area on the south side of river; paved boat ramp, parking on the north side. Tou Velle Park is the last take-out point for river drifters. The Rogue is free-flowing for another three miles to Gold Ray Dam, but only jet boats can make the trip.
Drift miles, measured from the hatchery ramp, are:

> **Casey Park:** 1
> **Rogue Elk Park:** 4
> **Shady Cove Park:** 10
> **Takelma Park:** 14
> **Dodge Bridge:** 18
> **Tou Velle Park:** 25

This section of the river is popular with tourists, as well as anglers, so there are many services for visitors. Shady Cove is the center of the tourist maelstrom and offers several motels, restaurants, RV parks, raft renters, and grocery stores. There are

a few general tackle suppliers, but no full-service fly shops. Fishin' Hole Tackle Shop and Deli has an excellent selection of trout and steelhead flies, leaders and other sundries, and some tying materials. Pat's Hand-Tied Flies (a few miles north of town) has a limited selection of flies.

All public parks in this section charge a day-use fee. You can buy an annual permit that is valid for county parks and Tou Velle State Park. It doesn't take too many days on the Rogue to justify buying an annual permit.

Upper Middle Rogue

The Upper Middle Rogue lies between Gold Ray Dam and Savage Rapids Dam. There isn't at lot of good fly water in this section. Also, roads are often rough, and private property restricts bank access. Hayes Falls and a diversion dam make boating treacherous between Gold Ray Dam and Gold Hill Park; drifters should not even attempt it. Some public access points are:

Bank access is provided by a rough, dirt road running 3.5 miles along the south side between Gold Ray Dam and Blackwell Rd.

While most of the land along John Day Rd. is private property, there is bank access near the dam.

October offers a mixed palette of golds and greens.

Hmm. Which fly do those fussy "Holy Water" trout want?

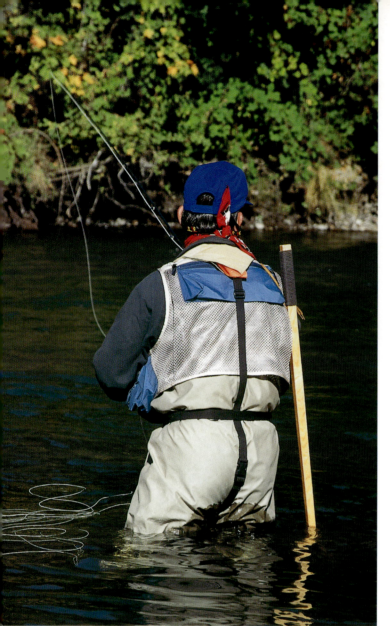
Looking for next best place.

Gold Nugget Recreation Area. Three picnic areas along SR 234 with unconnected bank access at each one; day-use only.

Gold Hill Park. Along SR 234. Paved ramp and bank access downstream from ramp; day-use only.

Sardine Creek. On North River Rd. Very rough (4x4 only) access to a dirt boat ramp. Some bank access (go upstream).

Valley of the Rogue State Park. On North River Rd. A large, well-maintained facility along the river within spitting (and hearing) distance of I-5. It has what you'd expect from an Oregon State Park: a boat ramp, camping, RV hookups, lots of green grass, hot showers, flush toilets, high cost, summer crowds.

Coyote Evans Wayside/Dee's Landing. On the south bank where the bridge crosses to US 99. Boat ramp, a few tables.

Fleming Rest Stop. Just downstream from Coyote Evans. Toilets, tables; day-use only.

Savage Rapids Park. On US 99 in Grants Pass. Paved ramp (not usable in low water).

As with the Upper Rogue, many public parks in this section charge a day-use fee. You can buy an annual permit that is valid for all county parks along the river.

Drift miles, measured from Gold Hill Park, are:
Sardine: 5
Valley of the Rogue State Park: 7
Coyote Evans Wayside: 9
Savage Rapids Park: 13

Grants Pass is a good-sized town with many motels, restaurants, and other services. Several RV parks are located on the river. A limited selection of fly tackle is available at Smith's Tackle Shop (3320 Redwood Highway).

Medford, the largest town in the region, is a half-hour drive from Grants Pass. Medford has most of the amenities a traveler could wish for. McKenzie Outfitters (130 E. 8th Street) has a full-service fly shop.

Ashland is a few more miles down I-5 from Medford. A full-service fly shop resides in the Ashland Outdoor Store (37 Third Street). The town's claim to fame is the Oregon Shakespeare Festival, one of the largest theater companies in the U.S. Plays run nine months of the year, so you can combine culture with fishing. I once had a fruitless day of winter steelheading—a day that included wind, rain, high water, no strikes, and a shuttle driver that left my truck three miles from where he was supposed to. That evening I went to Ashland and watched King Lear. It seemed a fitting end to the day.

Lower Middle Rogue

This section starts below Savage Rapids Dam in Grants Pass and ends at Grave Creek. Although public bank access is often a problem, there is some excellent fly fishing in Grants Pass, if you don't mind the sounds and sights of town. Below Grants Pass, the river is mostly flat and not good for fly fishing until you reach the Whitehorse area.

Salmon and steelhead bound for the upper river pass through here, and in fall the spring and fall chinook stack up near Grants Pass and begin spawning. This creates opportunities for steelheaders; see the section on Steelhead Tactics.

Grants Pass is a city of only 20,000 souls, so you don't have to go far to get out of town. Below Schroeder Park, the river has a rural feel, and by the time you reach the Hellgate area, it's quite wild. From Hog Creek to Grave Creek, the river is popular with whitewater boaters on day trips. The rapids are frequent, but all

Nymphing is a very effective method for Rogue steelhead.

38

are Class II and below, so this is a popular "splash-and-giggle" section in summer. However, hard boats should be cautious of the large boils in the narrow part of the Hellgate and near Morrison's Lodge.

Huge jet boats carry tourists through here in summer; after one of these noisy behemoths passes, fishing goes to hell for about an hour—just in time for the next big jet boat to come along. Between the jet boats and the rafters, fly fishers tend to avoid this section except at dawn and dusk and in the winter.

Some access points are described below. Unless stated otherwise, all are for day-use only.

Pierce Riffle Park (north bank). Paved ramp, paved trails, toilets.

Chinook Park (south bank). Off US 99. Paved ramp, tables, toilets.

Tom Pearce Park (north). Toilets, grassy area, baseball diamond, frisbee golf. Good bank access, but no ramp.

Baker Park (south). Where Park St. crosses US 199. Paved ramp, toilets.

Riverside Park (south). Corner of Park and Vista streets in Grants Pass. Family park with picnicking, toilets, play area, shade, baseball diamond; paved ramp at east end.

Water Restoration Plant (north). Take Bridge Rd. to Greenwood; at end of road. Bank access only, no facilities.

Tussing Park (south). Turn off US 199 onto Ringuette St. Take the gravel road where it says "Gate Ahead." Dirt parking lot, bank access; no other facilities.

Schroeder Park (south). Turn off US 199 onto Dowell Rd, then follow signs. Trailer parking, camping, RV hookups, play area, toilets, paved ramp.

There is dirt pull-out (north) off Lower River Road a mile and a quarter from Lincoln Rd.; it's opposite the Schroeder Park boat ramp. Bank access only.

Lathrop Boat Landing (north). On Lower River Road. Paved ramp.

Whitehorse County Park (north). Off Lower River Rd. Lots of shade, picnicking, camping with RV hookups, toilets, paved ramp, trail along river.

Matson Park (north). Off Lower River Rd. Gravel point from which boats could be launched; no other facilities.

Griffin Park (south). Off River Banks Rd. Camping, water, picnicking, play area, paved ramp.

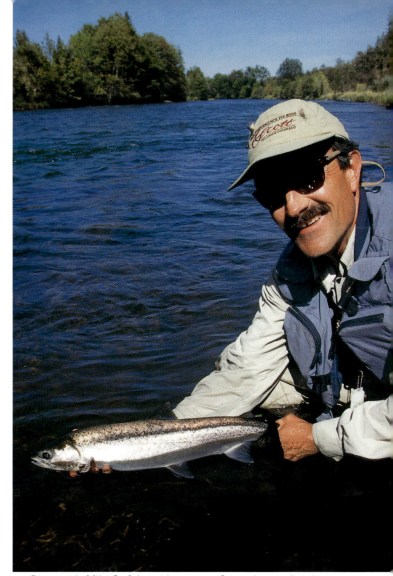

River guide Mike St. John with gorgeous September steelhead from the upper Rogue.

Ferry Park (north). At end of Ferry Rd. (follow signs) off Lower River Rd. Paved ramp; no other facilities.

Robertson Bridge (north). Paved ramp on east side of bridge, toilets.

Hog Creek. On Galice Rd. Paved ramp and raft staging area below, parking and toilets above (*way* above).

Stratton Creek Rd. is a spur off Galice Rd. It leads to bank access with toilets.

Indian Mary County Park. On Galice Rd. Camping, picnicking, play area, showers, dump station. Paved ramp.

Rainbow Recreation Site. Off Galice Rd. A gravel spur leads to river access. Toilets and a few tables, but otherwise primitive.

Ennis Riffle. Off Galice Rd. Paved ramp, toilets.

Carpenter's Island. Off Galice Rd. Gravel spur leads to short radius turnaround. Parking is a problem. No facilities.

Galice Creek. On Galice Rd. Pull-out near bridge over Galice Creek. Trail leads to river.

Galice Ramp. At the store. Public paved ramp, toilets.

Rocky Riffle Trail. On Galice Rd. Pull-out along road; walk to river.

Chair Riffle. Off Galice Rd. Steep, rough road leads to water. No facilities.

Rand. Off Galice Rd. Dirt ramp, toilets, tables.

Rand Visitor's Center. On Galice Rd. Forest Service/BLM

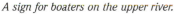

A sign for boaters on the upper river.

Humans are not the only ones who hunt the river's steelhead.
(Note fish tail in otter's mouth)

Most services for the Lower Middle Rogue will be found along the Grants Pass-Medford-Ashland axis (see previous section). Some services are available in Galice, which is more a community than a town. Galice's only store has a sign stating, "This is Galice," for confused newcomers who were expecting a city with more than one building. The store/restaurant does a brisk business in ice cream, sodas, beer, sweatshirts, and the miscellaneous items that boaters and tourists are likely to have forgotten or run out of. It is also a central point for arranging shuttles.

Merlin sits at the crossroads of Galice-Merlin Rd. and Robertson Bridge Rd., just upstream from Galice. You'll find several shops, including The Silver Sedge, a small, limited-hours fly shop.

Wild Rogue

Martin James put a finger to his lips, then pointed to our left. I stopped rowing the raft and looked. "Two otters," he whispered. "No, three. Tell a lie—there's four of them!" I quietly pulled the raft into a back eddy, and for the next twenty minutes we watched the otters and took photos of them. One of the playful mammals had a huge fish tail sticking out its mouth, evidently all that remained of a luckless steelhead. "I wouldn't have minded catching that fish myself," Martin said. "It probably went four pounds. But I'll gladly let the otters have it."

The next morning we found bear scat near our camp, and farther downstream a sandy beach bore the imprints of a black bear. "Yeah," said one camper we passed, "we found bear tracks all across our rafts when we woke up. I guess we shouldn't have left that food out."

The 33-mile Wild Rogue section, which runs from Grave Creek to Foster Bar, abounds with wildlife. In addition to bears

building where you get permits and information for drifting the Wild Rogue.

Almeda Park. Off Galice Rd. Camping, tables, toilets. Paved ramp. This area, not Grave Creek, is the best staging place for a trip through the Wild Rogue.

Argo. Off Galice Rd. Steep paved road leads to gravel bar and dirt boat ramp; toilets.

Grave Creek. Steep, single-lane paved road to river. Paved ramp, limited parking and staging area. Trail into Wild Rogue starts here. On the south side of the bridge there is a trail that leads to Rainie Falls.

As with the Upper Rogue, many public parks in this section charge a day-use fee. You can buy an annual permit that is valid for all county parks along the river.

Drift miles, measured from Pierce Riffle, are:

> **Baker Park:** 5
> **Riverside Park:** 5
> **Schroeder Park:** 8
> **Lathrop Landing:** 9
> **Whitehorse Park:** 13
> **Ferry Park:** 17
> **Griffin Park:** 17
> **Robertson Bridge:** 20
> **Hog Creek:** 24
> **Indian Mary Park:** 26
> **Ennis Riffle:** 29
> **Galice Ramp:** 30
> **Rand:** 33
> **Almeda Park:** 34
> **Argo:** 36
> **Grave Creek:** 38

When autumn leaves are falling, head for the river.

A rafter negotiates rapids above Rainie Falls.

and otters, you may spot deer, bald eagles, herons, kingfishers, mink, and many other animals. This section was one of the original eight "wild and scenic" rivers designated by Congress. The designation is intended to keep the river "free of impoundments and generally accessible only by trail," with "vestiges of primitive America."

The Rogue cuts through the coastal mountains here, creating a beautiful, rock-ribbed canyon that compresses the river as it drops to the ocean. The Rogue is actually narrower here than it is farther upstream. As you might expect, the combination of a narrow river, a steeper gradient, and rocky topography makes for serious whitewater, and expert boaters come from all over the U.S. to take on Blossom Bar, Mule Creek Canyon, and other gut-wrenchers. This stretch of river boasts 33 Class II rapids, 9 Class IIIs, 3 Class IVs, and one Class V (Rainie Falls); fortunately, you can line your boat around Rainie Falls. Make no mistake: this is serious whitewater. One rapids, Blossom Bar, eats several dozen driftcraft every year. Boaters need to have advanced skills if they intend to enter this area without a guide.

For those who don't float the Wild Rogue, there is a trail that parallels the north bank, but there is no road access. Bankside camping is available in many places, and there are several rustic lodges for those seeking soft beds and a roof.

Fly fishing in this section can be good, but you have to pick your water carefully; usually it is either too fast or too slow for good fly fishing. Another problem with fishing here is the river traffic. Because the canyon is narrow (on average, about half the width of the sections upstream), there are few places where passing boats will not run over your water. Also, this is a popular section for driftboat guides with gear-fishing clients. Most of them are a polite lot, but there are a few who think nothing of rowing right over the top of your fly.

The Wild Rogue is the most popular section of the river. To keep some semblance of its wild character, the BLM and Forest Service (joint managers of this section) let a maximum of 120 people start down the river each day between May 15 and October 15. To obtain a non-commercial permit, write to the Rand Visitor's Center, 14335 Galice Rd, Merlin, OR 97532; or call 541/479-3735. Permits are allocated on a lottery system, so you don't always get the dates you want. However, if you lose out on the lottery, you may be able to get the permit of someone who didn't show up on their day; check at the Rand Visitor's Center, and they will tell you what to do.

There are numerous established campsites along the Wild Rogue. The Rand Visitor's Center can give you a list of them. Campers should stay at sites with toilets. In fact, some of the sites are running out of places to dig holes for new outhouses, and it's expected that visitors will soon be required to carry portable potties and pack out their waste.

As for the bears . . . the Rogue's black bears have yet to eat an angler, or even seriously pummel one. However, they can be a nuisance and can cause major damage to your camping equipment. The biggest bear problems are below Paradise Bar. To avoid trouble, don't leave food around, leave no scraps at the camp, and *never* store food in your tent, or even keep toothpaste, cooking gear, or other odorous and attractive items near your sleeping area. Some of the campsites have enclosures with electric fences; you should have no problems if you store your food and cooking equipment in there. The Rand Visitor's Center can tell you where the problem areas are and what precautions you should take.

If bears and camping are not your style, there are several rustic lodges that host travelers on the Wild Rogue. Most are

Current regulations for the upper river during September and October allow for fly fishing only.

only open during the May to October peak season. Be sure to make a reservation well in advance of your trip. Lodges are:

Black Bar. 10 miles below Grave Creek. 541/479-6507.

Marial. 20 miles below Grave Creek. 541/474-2057.

Paradise. 24 miles below Grave Creek (below Blossom Bar); open all year. 800/525-2161.

Half Moon Bar. 24 miles below Grave Creek; open all year. 541/247-6968.

Clay Hill. 29 miles below Grave Creek. 800/228-3198 ext. 8235.

Wild River. 31 miles below Grave Creek. 800/228-3198 ext. 8235.

Lower Rogue

Some kind of anadromous fish can be found here at any time of year. However, the chinook salmon (both spring and fall) are too big and fresh for fly rodders; as one expert put it, "they'll either spool ya, tow ya out to sea, or a sea lion will get 'em." And winter steelheading is iffy because frequent winter storms are always blowing the river out of shape. And the summer steelhead tend to travel through very quickly and not hold up; when it's good, it's incredible, but it can change from fantastic to horrible overnight.

But then there are the half-pounders. The "Rogue rascals" are thick in the river from mid-August through fall, and they provide excellent fly fishing. Most fly anglers concentrate their efforts between Illahee and Agness. Below Agness, non-flyfishing gear is used to catch passing salmon and steelhead.

Public access is described below.

Above Agness, there is a road along the west bank. Above Coon Rock Bridge, it is narrow and there are places you can climb down to the river. At the north end, follow signs to reach the Rogue River Trailhead. Foster Bar (standard takeout for Wild Rogue drifters) has toilets and limited camping. A couple of miles below Foster Bar, Illahee is a pleasant but primitive campground with toilets, tables, and river access via trail (no boat ramp). Below Coon Rock Bridge, private property lessens river access. At the Agness end of the road, a privately-owned road gives public access (revocable for bad behavior) to a gravel bar from which a boat could be launched.

On the east bank above Agness, you'll find a dirt road next to Cougar Lane Resort. It leads to Cougar Lane Bar, a gravel bar from which a boat could be launched.

Between Gold Beach and Agness, the Agness Road gives access to the river's south bank. Boats can be launched from the large gravel bars. Camping is permitted only where indicated. Access points are:

Steelhead can be caught almost any month of the year.

Near its headwaters, the Rogue is a small mountain stream.

Bill Moore Creek. A gravel road leads to a primitive site with river access (no ramp) and a picnic table.

Quosatana. A very large campground with paved boat ramp and all campground amenities including an RV dump station.

Lobster Creek. Campground, picnic area, paved ramp, toilets. River access to large gravel bar.

Orchard Bar. Dirt road to large gravel bar. No facilities.

Huntley Park. Private campground and public access to large gravel bar.

Coyote Bar. Rough dirt road overhung with alders and squeezed by blackberry vines; leads to large gravel bar. No facilities.

Plywood Mill. Dirt road leads to large gravel bar. No facilities; day-use only.

North Bank Road gives access to the river's north bank. The road is paved in its lower reaches, but private property severely limits river access (it's not great fly water, anyway). Above Lobster Creek, it becomes a single-lane dirt road. You could bushwhack to the river (but why?). Some spurs lead to gravel bars from which boats could be launched. After awhile, follow signs for Lower Rogue River Trail at the end of the road; the trail gives access to the river (dodge the cows and cow pies). Be respectful of private property where encountered. The dirt road is subject to washouts.

The lower end of North Bank Road has two public boat launch points: Canfield Bar (gravel bar; no facilities) and a paved ramp half a mile from the junction with Edson Rd (very limited parking).

The town of Gold Beach sits where the Rogue empties into the sea. Tackle dealers include the Rogue Outdoor Store (560 N. Highway 101; 541/247-7142). Master fly-tier Al Brunell operates the Golden Demon Fly Den out of his basement. It has more fly-tying stuff than you'll see at most large shops. It is a limited-hours store, so call first (541/247-6916) to make sure Al is there and to get directions.

In summer, Gold Beach hosts swarms of tourists traveling the Oregon Coast. While there are plenty of motels, make reservations during the height of the August tourist season or you'll find slim pickings. (On an August evening almost thirty years ago, my wife and I traveled through here on our honeymoon. We ended up in one of the last two rooms in town, an unswept hovel with a sagging mattress and a bathroom of questionable hygiene. It's still a source of jokes.)

The Applegate and Illinois Rivers

The Rogue is joined by two major tributaries, the Applegate and Illinois Rivers. Each supports significant runs of fall chinook and winter steelhead, but each can be difficult to fish for widely different reasons.

The Applegate is the gentler of the two tributaries. It is surrounded by private property for almost its entire length, and the river is unsuited for boating (trust me on this; I've tried it).

In death as in life, wild salmon enrich the river.

However, there are several places were you can park your car and find a good fishing spot. Try the area near the junction of Fish Hatchery Road and Southside Road. Also, just east of Murphy there is good access to extensive bank fishing. Near Provolt there is another spot.

For the most part, the Applegate is a shallow, gentle river. The best fishing is in slots and occasional deep pools. It is water that is better suited to a deep-drifted fly (see the section on Steelhead Tactics) than a swung fly.

The Illinois is completely different than the Applegate. The river is not especially broad, but it is deep—often 15 to 20 feet—and heavily bouldered. While many of the mid-river rocks are about the size of Volkswagens, many others are as big as three Buicks piled oil-pan to rooftop. And there are sudden falls and major rapids.

As you might expect, boating the Illinois is a challenge. In fact, the wilderness section of the Illinois has some of the toughest and most remote whitewater in the lower 48 states. In 31 miles, boaters encounter over 30 Class III rapids, 12 Class IVs, and a V or two. Most of this section runs through a 4,000-foot-deep canyon with no road or trail, so if you get in trouble you are in deep do-do indeed. Further, the Illinois is a spate river,

and a heavy rain can raise the water level by three feet in one day, rendering rapids unpassable. More than one Illinois boating party has had to wait in one place for a couple of days while the river dropped back to a runnable state. Needless to say, it takes expert whitewater skills to handle almost any part of the Illinois, especially the wilderness section. On the other hand, you'll have a hard time finding a more remote spot in Oregon. Fewer than 70 boating parties a year travel through the wilderness stretch. The best months are February through April.

Not all of the Illinois is as inaccessible as the wilderness section. Illinois River Road (turn at the Selma Market) parallels part of the river. Find a turnout, scramble down to the river (probably a fast 500-foot elevation drop). Crawl over huge rocks and cliffs looking for likely fishing places; try not to slip and bash your head or drown. Once you find good water, figure out how you can make your fly reach the winter steelhead, who are hugging the bottom in 20 feet of water. Contemplate the wheezing ascent back to your car.

Sound tough? It is. But the Illinois supports a good run of winter steelhead, most of them over 12 pounds and all of them wild native fish. Bait is not allowed, and all fish must be released. Few fly anglers go here, and even fewer are successful.

Trout can be found in the headwaters section.

Wildflowers herald summer fishing on the upper Rogue.

Some end up wishing wistfully for a couple of slinkies and a gob of salmon roe.

If you're feeling a little out of shape, spend a winter fishing and boating the Illinois every day. At the end of the season, you'll be ready to take on Arnold Schwarzenegger.

Regulations

Due to its diversity of species, the Rogue River has angling regulations so complex they make you wish your fishing partner was a lawyer. Current (1999) regulations are summarized below by river section. The final authority, of course, is the official Oregon Sport Fishing Regulations synopsis, available at most Oregon tackle dealers.

Headwaters (Above Lost Creek Reservoir)

Open from fourth Saturday in April to October 31

Five trout over eight inches may be kept each day; no limit on brook trout

"Holy Water"(Between Lost Creek Dam and hatchery diversion dam—about one mile)

open all year

fly-fishing-only with barbless hooks

all fish must be released unharmed

Upper Rogue
(Hatchery diversion dam to Gold Ray Dam)

from hatchery diversion dam to markers (including hatchery outflow), closed to all angling

open for trout January 1 to March 31, and fourth Saturday in May to December 31; up to two adipose-clipped rainbow trout per day, eight-inch minimum; release all cutthroat trout

rainbow trout over 16 inches are considered steelhead

open for fin-clipped coho salmon September 1 to December 31

September 1 to October 31, fly fishing only

open for chinook salmon and steelhead all year, except closed to chinook angling from August 1 to October 31

non-adipose-clipped steelhead at least 24 inches in length may be kept: one per day, five per year (state-wide) from February 1 to April 30

up to two adult salmon or steelhead (in combination) may be kept each day

fly-fishing-only September and October

Upper Middle Rogue
(Gold Ray Dam to Savage Rapids Dam)

Same as Upper Rogue, except:

no fly-only season

closed to chinook angling October 1 to December 31

closed to all angling from Gold Ray Dam downstream to markers below lowest fishway entrance

closed to all angling from Ideal Cement Co. Powerhouse diversion dam downstream to Gold Hill boat landing

Ride'em cowboy! A cataraft sets up to run Rainie Falls.

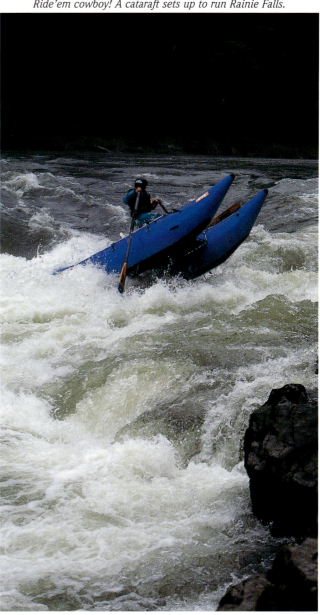

As green changes to gold, fall anglers know their time is short.

Lower Middle Rogue
(Savage Rapids Dam to Grave Creek)

Same as Upper Rogue, except:

no fly-only season

October 1 to December 31, closed to chinook angling from Hog Creek boat landing to Savage Rapids dam

closed to all angling from Savage Rapids dam to markers below lowest fishway entrance

Wild Rogue (Grave Creek to Foster Bar)

Same as Upper Rogue, except:

no fly-only season

closed to all angling from Rainie Falls downstream 400 feet

Lower Rogue (Foster Bar to tidewater)

Same as Upper Rogue, except:

no fly-only season

one chinook salmon may be kept per day (5 per year) from mouth to Illinois River, October 1 to December 31

Other Resources

The Chambers of Commerce in the Rogue River area will send you a vacation packet that includes information about RV parks, motels, and other visitor information. For Josephine County (Lower Middle Rogue, Wild Rogue; Grants Pass) call 541/476-7717. For Jackson County (Upper Rogue, Upper Middle Rogue; Medford, Ashland, Shady Cove) call 541/779-4847. For Curry County (Lower Rogue; Gold Beach) call 541/247-7526.

Shuttles. If you're drifting the river, you need a shuttle driver. These services are a cottage industry for locals, but the suppliers tend to come and go. Therefore, check with local fishing and rafting shops to find out who is providing reliable services this year. For the Upper Rogue, Upper Middle, and Lower Middle Rogue, check with Ashland Outdoor Store, McKenzie Outfitters, or Fishin' Hole (See below for phone numbers). On the Upper River, I use TZ Shuttle Service (541/826-2526). For the Wild Rogue, call the Galice store (541/476-3818). On the Lower Rogue, call Laverne Parry (541/247-6778 or 800/207-7886).

Guides. Fly-fishing guides can be arranged through Ashland Outdoor Store, McKenzie Outfitters, and Fishin' Hole (see below for phone numbers). For a pamphlet listing all Oregon guides, including those who will take you through the Wild Rogue section, contact the Oregon Guides and Packers Association, PO Box 10841, Eugene, OR 97440.

Maps and Guide Books.

Handbook to the Rogue River Canyon (Frank Amato Publications, Portland, Oregon). A detailed guide and history for those running the Wild Rogue. Available at most area fishing and rafting stores.

The Rogue River Guide (Mountain N'Air Books, La Crescenta, California). The Lower Middle and Wild Rogue from a kayaker's perspective. Available at most rafting suppliers.

Rogue River Float Guide. A joint publication of the Bureau of Land Management and the US Forest Service that summarizes the Wild Rogue. Available at rafting suppliers or from the Rand office.

Streamline (Redding, California) has an accurate and useful map of the entire Rogue except the Wild section.

Useful Phone Numbers

Upper Rogue information (inflow and outflow from Lost Creek and Applegate dams; 1,500 cfs is a typical flow): 800/472-2434

Rand Visitor's Center (Wild Rogue permits): 541/479-3735

Grants Pass weather and river information (river level, temperature, and flow at the Grants Pass Water Filtration Plant; 2,500 to 3,000 cfs is typical flow): 541/476-5256

Oregon Department of Fish and Wildlife Fish Line (fishing reports from around the state): 800/275-3474

Ashland Outdoor Store (fly shop in Ashland): 541/488-1202

McKenzie Outfitters (fly shop in Medford): 541/247-6916

Fishin' Hole (some fly supplies in Shady Cove): 541/878-4000

Golden Demon Fly Den (fly shop in Gold Beach): 541/247-6916

Silver Sedge (fly shop in Merlin): 541/476-2456